MAKING ROBOT WARRIORS FROM JUNK

MAKING ROBOT WARRIORS FROM JUNK

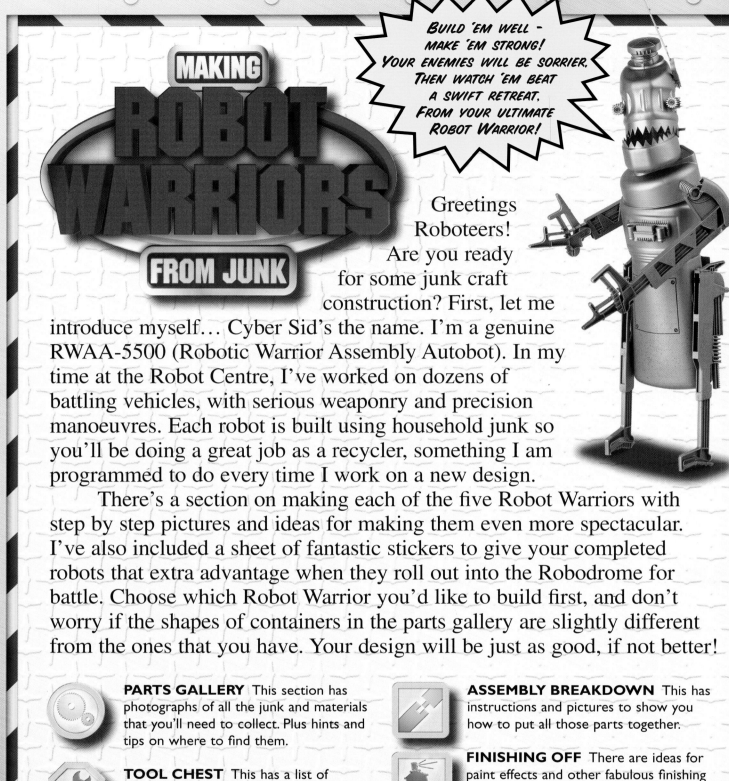

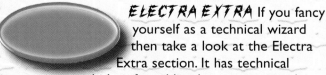

> BUILD 'EM WELL –
> MAKE 'EM STRONG!
> YOUR ENEMIES WILL BE SORRIER,
> THEN WATCH 'EM BEAT
> A SWIFT RETREAT,
> FROM YOUR ULTIMATE
> ROBOT WARRIOR!

Greetings Roboteers! Are you ready for some junk craft construction? First, let me introduce myself… Cyber Sid's the name. I'm a genuine RWAA-5500 (Robotic Warrior Assembly Autobot). In my time at the Robot Centre, I've worked on dozens of battling vehicles, with serious weaponry and precision manoeuvres. Each robot is built using household junk so you'll be doing a great job as a recycler, something I am programmed to do every time I work on a new design.

There's a section on making each of the five Robot Warriors with step by step pictures and ideas for making them even more spectacular. I've also included a sheet of fantastic stickers to give your completed robots that extra advantage when they roll out into the Robodrome for battle. Choose which Robot Warrior you'd like to build first, and don't worry if the shapes of containers in the parts gallery are slightly different from the ones that you have. Your design will be just as good, if not better!

PARTS GALLERY This section has photographs of all the junk and materials that you'll need to collect. Plus hints and tips on where to find them.

TOOL CHEST This has a list of recommended tools, together with hints on how to use them safely.

HAZARD WARNING These highlight important safety precautions, and tasks that require adult help. Remember a good Roboteer always puts safety first!

TOP TIPS Get off to a flying start with the best tips from our top technicians at the Robot Centre. So check out the hottest hints on construction techniques.

ASSEMBLY BREAKDOWN This has instructions and pictures to show you how to put all those parts together.

FINISHING OFF There are ideas for paint effects and other fabulous finishing touches, including the best places to position your stickers to make your robot the coolest in the Robodrome.

ELECTRA EXTRA If you fancy yourself as a technical wizard then take a look at the Electra Extra section. It has technical instructions and ideas for adding battery-powered motors, lights and buzzers to your Robot Warriors. There are also instructions for building a superb remote control. You'll need the help of a friendly adult, but if you're a budding bright spark have a go!

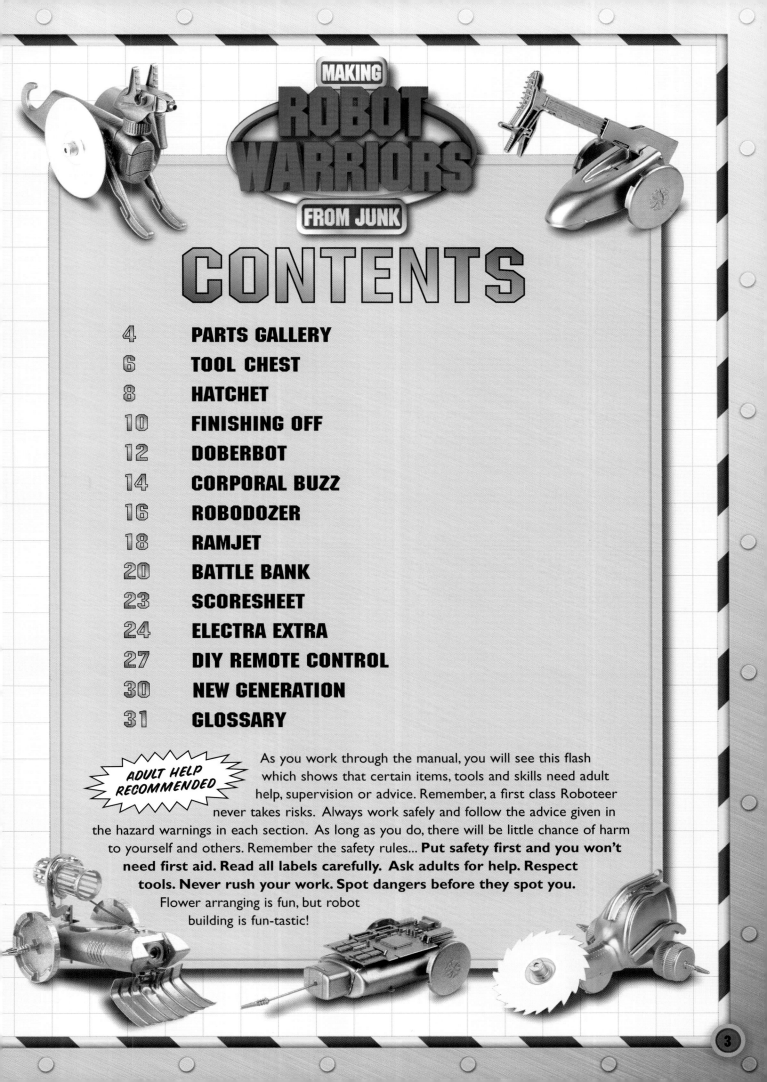

MAKING ROBOT WARRIORS FROM JUNK

CONTENTS

ADULT HELP RECOMMENDED

As you work through the manual, you will see this flash which shows that certain items, tools and skills need adult help, supervision or advice. Remember, a first class Roboteer never takes risks. Always work safely and follow the advice given in the hazard warnings in each section. As long as you do, there will be little chance of harm to yourself and others. Remember the safety rules... **Put safety first and you won't need first aid. Read all labels carefully. Ask adults for help. Respect tools. Never rush your work. Spot dangers before they spot you.** Flower arranging is fun, but robot building is fun-tastic!

PARTS GALLERY

Before you start, make sure you ask an adult for permission to help yourself to junk around the house. You'll find a shoe box or grocery carton is ideal to store all your parts and tools in one place. Ask relatives and friends for junk— that way, you'll be encouraging them to recycle too.

Baking powder or soda tubs

Circular air fresheners pulled apart make fantastic wheels

Wedge shaped air freshener

Talcum powder bottles

Large water bottles

Small water bottles with pop-up caps

Screw-top lids come in all different sizes and colours

Pop-up caps from drink bottles

Paper fasteners

Shower gel bottles with moulded hooks

Shower gel bottles with a flip hook

⚠ HAZARDS

- CHECK THE HAZARD WARNING PANELS BEFORE STARTING ANY PROJECTS. IF YOU ARE UNSURE ABOUT ANYTHING, ASK AN ADULT.
- SOME CONTAINERS CONTAIN HARMFUL SUBSTANCES SUCH AS BLEACH. ALWAYS CHECK WITH AN ADULT IF IT IS SAFE TO USE THEM.
- ASK AN ADULT TO WASH USED TOILET FRESHENER HOLDERS IN VERY HOT WATER!
- REFER TO THE TOP TIPS PANEL OPPOSITE FOR IDEAS ON WHERE TO FIND OLD COMPUTER CIRCUIT BOARDS. REMEMBER, YOU SHOULD NEVER HANDLE ELECTRICAL EQUIPMENT THAT IS STILL IN USE OR PLUGGED IN TO MAINS ELECTRICITY.

Cardboard can be cut into shapes such as saw blades

Dressmaker's elastic cord

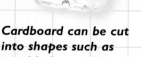

Shower gel bottles with flip-top lids

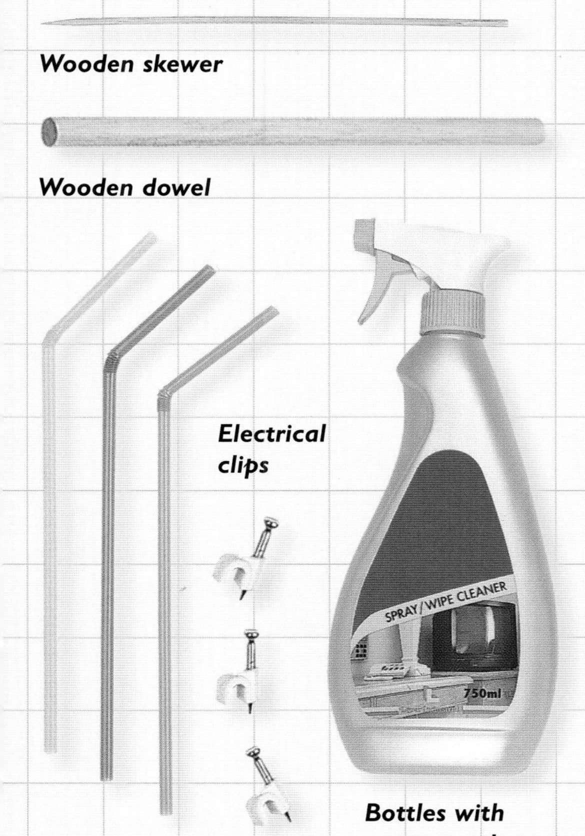

Wooden skewer

Wooden dowel

Electrical clips

● To modify robots for running on smooth, slippery surfaces, stretch small, wide elastic bands or a length of draught-proofing door strip around the wheel rims for extra grip.

● Wall plugs should be the kind used for putting screws in walls. They look just the part as far as wheel spikes go.

● You can get hold of old circuit boards quite easily from any store that upgrades computers. They will probably have a whole box full of broken or out-of-date sound cards, video cards and modems. You may have a circuit board at home already if someone in the house upgrades their own computer from time to time. But be sure to ask for permission before gluing someone's brand new memory chips onto the back of Ramjet!

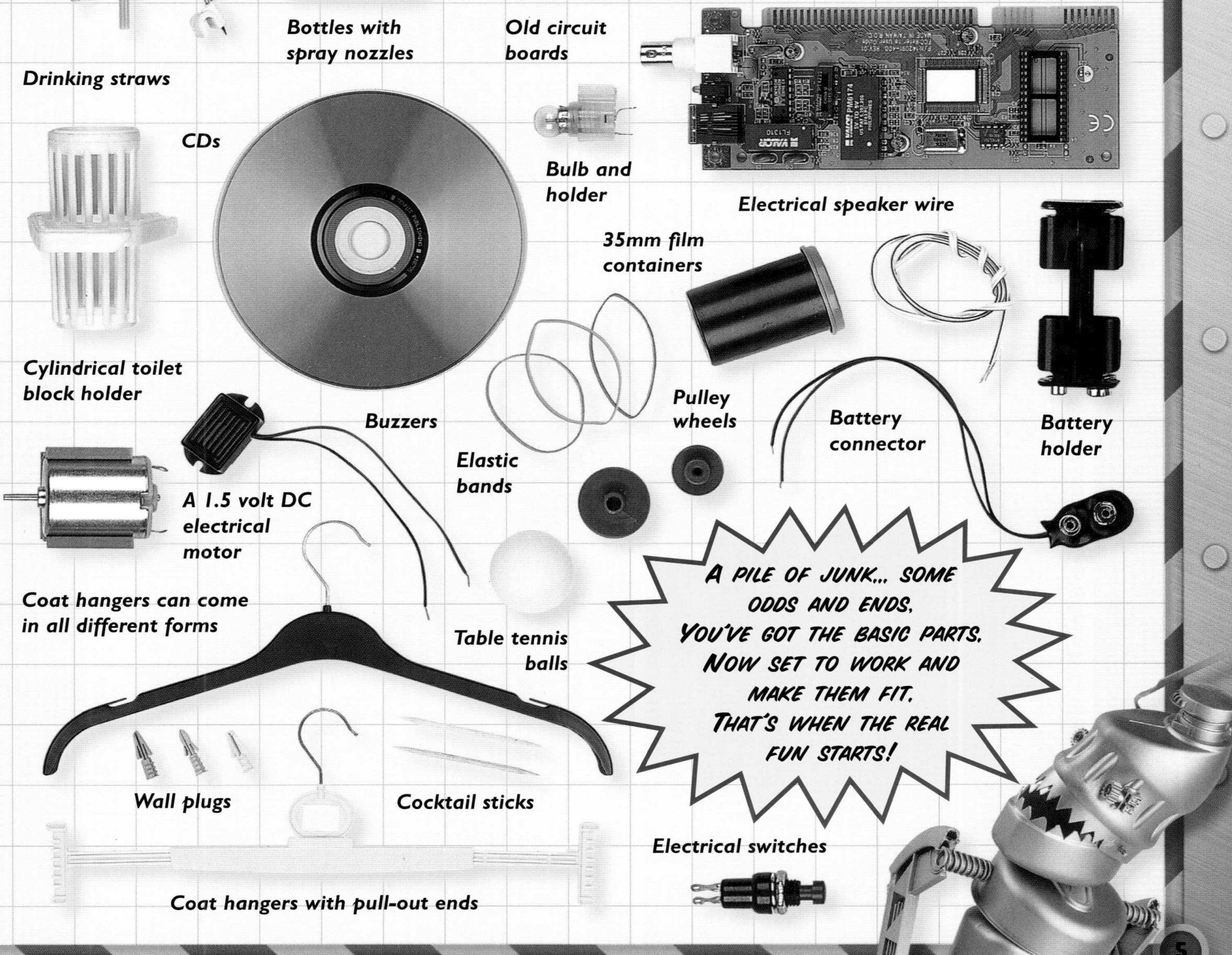

SPRAY/WIPE CLEANER

750ml

Bottles with spray nozzles

Old circuit boards

Drinking straws

CDs

Bulb and holder

Electrical speaker wire

35mm film containers

Cylindrical toilet block holder

Buzzers

Pulley wheels

Battery connector

Battery holder

Elastic bands

A 1.5 volt DC electrical motor

Coat hangers can come in all different forms

Table tennis balls

A PILE OF JUNK... SOME ODDS AND ENDS, YOU'VE GOT THE BASIC PARTS, NOW SET TO WORK AND MAKE THEM FIT, THAT'S WHEN THE REAL FUN STARTS!

Wall plugs

Cocktail sticks

Electrical switches

Coat hangers with pull-out ends

TOOL CHEST

Although just a few simple tools are needed for these projects, you may find others that are very useful. Always ask an adult before you use a tool and check if it is safe to use on your own.

You'll find you work better if you keep all your tools together in a clearly marked box. Make sure that saws, knives and sharp tools are stowed safely so you won't cut yourself when you get them out. Saws and knives are safer if they are kept clean and sharp–a blunt, dirty edge is more likely to slip.

SCISSORS (LARGE AND SMALL)

Scissors are very handy for all sorts of jobs, but always take care with the sharp blades.

PLIERS

Great for twisting wires together in the Electra Extra section – a small pair of long-nose pliers is ideal.

BRADAWL

A hot bradawl is best for making round holes. If you don't have one, use an old knitting needle.

JUNIOR HACKSAW

Fix the object in a vice or hold it firmly over the edge of a bench. Keep the saw upright and cut on the push-stroke (you shouldn't need to push hard), using the whole length of the saw.

MARKER PEN

Choose one which will write on plastic.

CRAFT KNIVES

Craft knives must be sharp so you don't need to press hard to cut. If you have to press hard there is more chance that your hand will slip.

SOLDERING IRON

Great for fixing wires in place, but you MUST have adult help if you use them because they get very hot.

NIGHTLIGHTS

Use these to heat a bradawl or craft knife to make holes or cuts in plastic.

WIPE CL
Bry
EXTRA LONG MATCHES

SHARP BLADES AND SPIKES - AND HOT TOOLS TOO TREAT THEM RIGHT, RESPECT IS DUE ALWAYS PUT YOUR SAFETY FIRST WITH HAZARD WARNINGS - BE WELL VERSED!

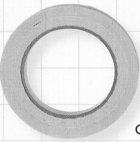

ELECTRICAL TAPE

Available at all DIY stores. You'll need this to join wires together in the Electra Extra section!

ARTISTS' PAINTBRUSHES

These can be bought at any art shop and come in various sizes. Good for spot painting – see Finishing Off, pages 10–11.

PAINT MASK

Available at most DIY store. You MUST wear one of these if you are spray-painting your robots.

ACRYLIC PAINT

Many colours are available from art shops. Ideal for spot painting plastic surfaces on robots, see Finishing Off, pages 10–11.

MASKING TAPE

Ideal for masking off parts of your robots you don't want to paint! See Finishing Off, pages 10–11.

SPRAY PAINT

Great for applying large areas of colour. ALWAYS wear a paint mask when using spray paint!

RUBBER GLOVES

Use for hot tool tasks, gluing and spray painting. You can buy them in supermarkets.

HAZARDS

- ALWAYS FOLLOW SAFETY RULES AND WARNINGS – EVEN SIMPLE TOOLS CAN BE DANGEROUS IF YOU ARE NOT CAREFUL WHEN USING THEM. REMEMBER CYBER SID'S RHYME.
- ALWAYS STORE CRAFT KNIVES, SAWS AND SCISSORS IN A SAFE PLACE WHEN NOT IN USE.
- MAKE SURE YOU WORK OUTSIDE OR IN A WELL–VENTILATED ROOM WHEN YOU ARE USING CONTACT ADHESIVE.
- IF YOU LIGHT A NIGHTLIGHT TO HEAT YOUR BRADAWL, NEVER LEAVE IT UNATTENDED.
- STAND TOOLS, SUCH AS YOUR BRADAWL, ON A HEAT RESISTANT SURFACE AND KEEP A TUB OF COLD WATER NEARBY TO DIP IT INTO SO IT COOLS DOWN QUICKLY.
- IF YOU NEED TO CHANGE YOUR HACKSAW BLADE ASK AN ADULT TO HELP YOU. REMEMBER TO SET THE NEW BLADE WITH ITS CUTTING TEETH POINTING FORWARDS – SAWS CUT AS YOU PUSH FORWARDS, NOT AS YOU PULL BACK.

GLUE

The best option is a solvent-free contact adhesive. Always read the instructions on the packet. See the Hazards panel.

PHILLIPS SCREWDRIVER

For making axle holes, see Ramjet and Hatchet.

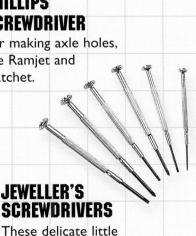

JEWELLER'S SCREWDRIVERS

These delicate little screwdrivers may come in handy for the Electra Extra section.

HATCHET

With its sleek, streamlined body, this Robot Warrior is nippy and manoeuvrable. A smooth-running ball wheel at the front means that the Hatchet can compete in the most challenging races and obstacle courses. Put that together with the powerful action of its hatchet arm and you have a winning combination.

PARTS

A wedge-shaped air freshener

2 circular stick-on air fresheners

2 electrical clips

1 plastic coat hanger similar to the one shown

Table tennis ball

A short length of wooden dowel

A wooden skewer

1 wooden cocktail stick or toothpick

TOOLS

- A junior hacksaw
- Bradawl or an old knitting needle
- Craft knife
- Scissors
- A Phillips screwdriver that is slightly thicker than the wooden dowel
- A nightlight
- Glue

CHECK OUT THE ELECTRA EXTRA SECTION BEFORE YOU START IF YOU WOULD LIKE TO FIT A MOTOR TO HATCHET TO MAKE HIM WHIZZ ALONG!

YOU CAN BASH 'EM - YOU CAN CRASH 'EM - SO GET READY FOR SOME FUN. KEEP YOUR GRANNY SAFELY LOCKED IN DOORS... WHEN HATCHET'S ON THE RUN.

HAZARD

- TAKE GREAT CARE WITH THE HOT BRADAWL ON STEPS 2 AND 9, AND THE HOT CRAFT KNIFE ON STEP 8!

ASSEMBLY

1 Push a small hole through the centre of the table tennis ball using the bradawl or knitting needle. Heat the bradawl first to make a perfectly round hole. Check the ball spins freely on the toothpick.

2 Pierce tiny holes through either side of the front end of the wedge-shaped air freshener, so the toothpick fits tightly. Your holes should be close to the edge and about 3cm from the front of the air freshener so the table tennis ball can spin freely.

3 Push the toothpick through the ball and the holes you have made. Snip off the ends of the toothpick using a strong pair of scissors. If you made the holes too large by mistake, then a small blob of glue will keep the toothpick in place.

Add blobs of glue if necessary to keep axle in place

4 Pull apart the air fresheners and take the two matching sides with larger holes. These will make the rear wheels. Cut a length of dowel about 4cm longer than the width of your wedge-shaped air freshener.

Approx. 9cm

Holes through either side of body

5 Heat your Phillips screwdriver and make holes through the sides of the body, about 3cm from the back and 1cm up from the edge. Adjust the holes so your dowel turns freely. Assemble the rear wheels as shown, using electrical clips to stabilise them. Check the robot rolls smoothly.

Electricians plastic clips

Glue wheels to the dowel if necessary

6 To make the hatchet, cut off one arm at least 22cm long from the plastic coat hanger using your hacksaw.

22cm

4cm

7 Pierce a hole through the hatchet arm, about 4cm from the back using your heated bradawl. Make sure the hole is large enough for the wooden skewer to fit through easily.

8 Using a warmed craft knife, cut a slot in the top of the robot as shown. The slot should be about 2cm wide, and 8cm long (4cm forwards from the back edge, and 4cm down).

9 Make a hole through the top corners of the robot body with a heated bradawl.

10 Attach the arm by slotting the wooden skewer through the holes you have made. Do make sure that the arm is facing downwards. Finally cut off the rest of the skewer with a hacksaw or strong scissors.

If you made the holes too big, add blobs of glue to the ends of the skewer.

Check that the arm can be flipped

11 Check that the arm can be easily flipped up with your thumb, whilst holding the robot firmly in the other hand. The arm should then fall back down with ease. Congratulations, Roboteer! You have successfully constructed a first-class Robot Warrior. Turn over for some finishing off ideas and tips.

FINISHING OFF

TOOLS

- Rubber gloves
- Paint mask
- Masking tape
- Paintbrushes
- Cans of spray paint and pots of paint

Car spray paints are ideal for adding sparkle to your robots. But be careful because the paint comes out in a fine mist which will settle on anything within close range. Hang your robot on a washing line with a bit of thin string. (But not on wash day!) Remove the lid and shake, shake, shake to make the metal ball rattle! Count to at least one hundred as you shake. Point the can away from you, with the nozzle about 20cm away from your robot. Once the paint has set completely, decorate your robots with model paints, stickers, designs from your computer's paint programme or pictures from magazines.

⚠ HAZARD

- WHEN SPRAY PAINTING, WEAR A PAINT MASK, OLD CLOTHES AND RUBBER GLOVES.
- ALWAYS SPRAY AWAY FROM YOURSELF AND OTHER PEOPLE.

TOP TIPS

- You'll get a smoother finish if you use short, sharp bursts of spray paint.
- Keep moving around your robot so that you spray it from all directions.
- Let the paint dry before you go over it again or blobs of runny paint will build up.
- If you do get blobs, let them dry, scrape them off with a craft knife and spray the whole robot again.
- Let your robot dry for at least 3 hours. Handling it too soon will cause the paint to peel and rub away.

Take a pile of useless junk
Clean it up, wash out the gunk
With glue, saw and crafty knife
Now bring that pile of junk to life
Spinning wheels, a chopping arm
Designed to deal out utmost harm
Before you know it – you'll have got
A first-class Warrior Robot!

Here are some tips on painting techniques to help you decorate your robots before you add those funky stickers!

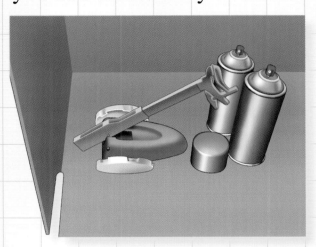

MAKING AND USING A SPRAY BOOTH

Hanging robots from the washing line is fine for sunny, calm days. If the weather is bad or you have to work indoors, make a spray booth. A large cardboard grocery box is ideal. Stand the box on its side with the flaps open. Put your robot near the back for spraying. Keep turning the robot to paint it all over.

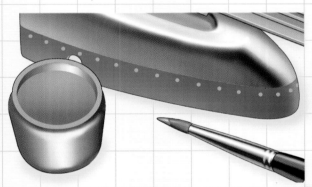

ADDING RIVETS AND BATTLE SCARS

Use a small brush to paint details such as rivets (above), and battles scars (below).

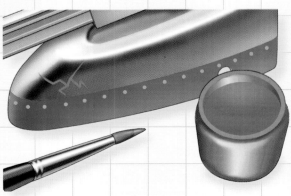

MASKING OFF

Use masking tape to create a two-tone effect. Press a strip of tape down firmly where you want a line. Smooth out kinks in the tape or the paint will 'bleed' under it and spoil your nice crisp line. Make sure the paint is dry before you remove the tape or it will smudge.

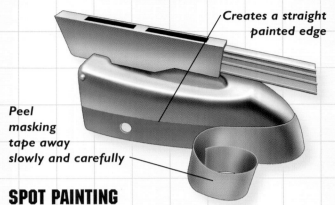

Creates a straight painted edge

Peel masking tape away slowly and carefully

SPOT PAINTING

Paint areas of your robot with a brush and contrasting colours to make them really stand out. Different parts of the body, wheels and weapons can all be different colours. If you make a mistake – just wipe it and start again.

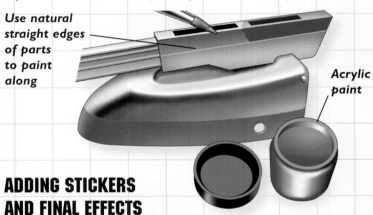

Use natural straight edges of parts to paint along

Acrylic paint

ADDING STICKERS AND FINAL EFFECTS

If all this talk of paint effects is bringing out the artist in you, then why not add exciting details to your robot such as ferocious teeth, glaring red eyes, claws, camouflage stripes or a lucky logo. A menacing look might even scare the opposition. Add the same kind of sticker on either side of your robot for a symmetrical, well-balanced look.

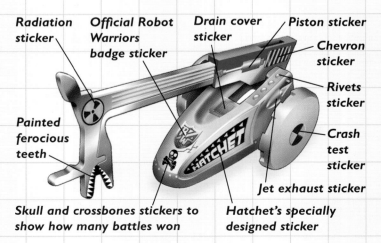

Radiation sticker

Official Robot Warriors badge sticker

Drain cover sticker

Piston sticker

Chevron sticker

Rivets sticker

Crash test sticker

Jet exhaust sticker

Painted ferocious teeth

Skull and crossbones stickers to show how many battles won

Hatchet's specially designed sticker

DOBERBOT

Two wheels are sometimes better than four and Doberbot can roll, spin, rock and perform a whole range of tricks on his two wheels. By controlling his tail you can even get him to scoop up the enemy with a flick from those powerful front paws.

Always alert, Doberbot's head can turn in any direction. He is forever on the lookout for intruders on his territory.

CHECK OUT THE ELECTRA EXTRA SECTION BEFORE YOU START IF YOU LIKE THE IDEA OF MAKING DOBERBOT'S EYES GLOW RED WITH RAGE!

TOOLS

- A junior hacksaw
- Bradawl or an old knitting needle
- Craft knife
- A nightlight
- Glue

HAZARD

- BE CAREFUL WHEN USING A HOT KNITTING NEEDLE ON STEP 3. IT'S BEST TO USE A PAIR OF PLIERS TO HOLD THE KNITTING NEEDLE.

PARTS

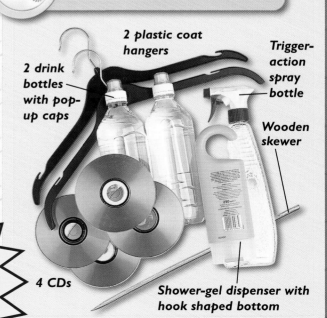

2 plastic coat hangers

2 drink bottles with pop-up caps

Trigger-action spray bottle

Wooden skewer

Shower-gel dispenser with hook shaped bottom

4 CDs

TEETH OF STEEL, LASER EYES
THIS ROBOT'S GOT THE LOT.
A BITE THAT'S MUCH
WORSE THAN HIS BARK,
OF COURSE... IT'S DOBERBOT!

1 To make the body, unscrew the tops from your two drink bottles and prise off the pop-up caps with a screwdriver or coin. Glue the two bottle tops to either side of the shower-gel container as shown.

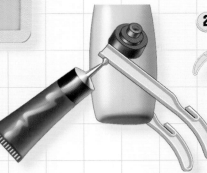

Saw the ends from coat hangers using a hacksaw. See Tools section for tips on sawing with a hacksaw

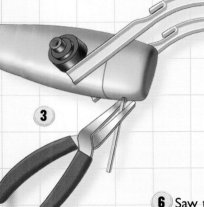

Keep the pop-up caps – you will need these later

2 Saw the ends from one of your coat hangers. About 16cm is long enough to make Doberbot's front legs. Rest the front legs on the bottle sections and glue them in place with a good squirt of glue.

5 Join Doberbot's head to his body through the holes you made earlier, cutting off the wooden skewer with strong scissors or hacksaw close to the body of the robot.

3 Heat a knitting needle in the nightlight flame. Hold it with a pair of pliers. Pierce a hole right through the shower-gel cap from one side to the other.

4 To make the head, unscrew the spray bottle top and pull off the plastic pipe that is attached to it. Glue your wooden skewer into the hole where the pipe was attached.

Doberbot's ears should be standing up tall and alert just like a real guard dog.

6 Saw the ends from your second coat hanger as shown, to form the ears. Glue the ears in place. All that remains is to decorate Doberbot with a lick of paint and decorate him with stickers.

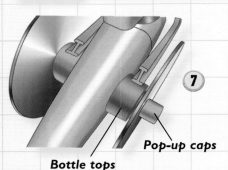

7 When you have painted Doberbot, put on the wheels. Place two CDs together for each wheel – shiny sides outwards. Press the pop-up caps firmly into position. Another spot of gluing may be necessary to make sure your bottle tops are secure. Finally decorate Doberbot with stickers.

Add Doberbot's specially designed sticker as shown.

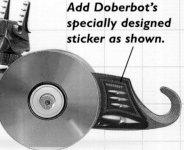

Pop-up caps

Bottle tops

CORPORAL BUZZ

With wide-tracked wheels, arching mudguards and an angled, razor-sharp saw blade, Corporal Buzz is designed to cope with the roughest terrain and anything that dares to get in his way. An armour-plated ridge gives strength to his body shell and rotating spikes on his wheels offer that extra element of surprise from the side.

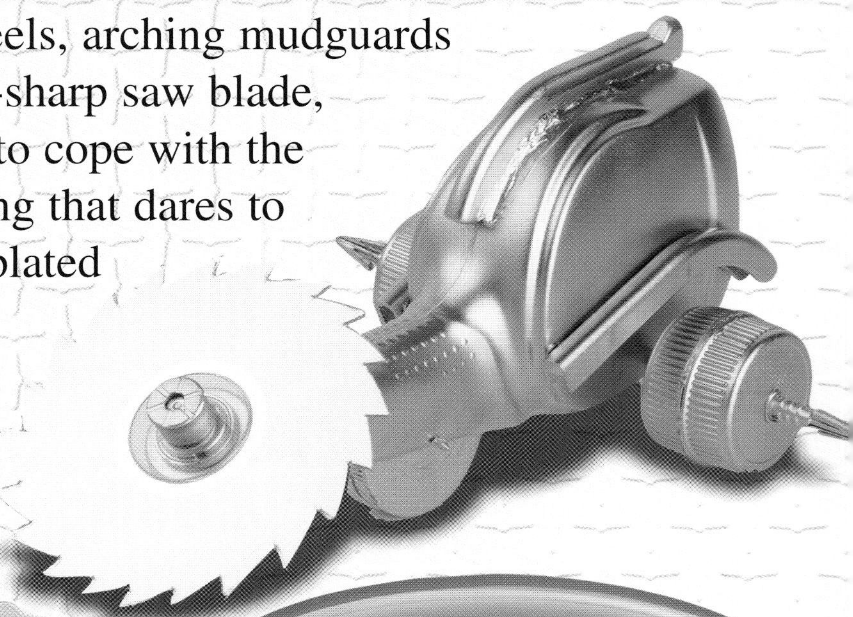

PARTS

1 trigger-action spray bottle
1 baking powder tub
1 wooden cocktail stick
1 drink bottle with pop-up cap
1 CD
4 large bottle tops
1 drinking straw
1 wooden skewer
2 plastic coat hangers
1 table tennis ball
2 wall plugs

CHECK OUT THE ELECTRA EXTRA SECTION TO FIND OUT HOW TO FIT A MOTOR. YOU'LL SOON HAVE THE CORPORAL BUZZING AROUND!

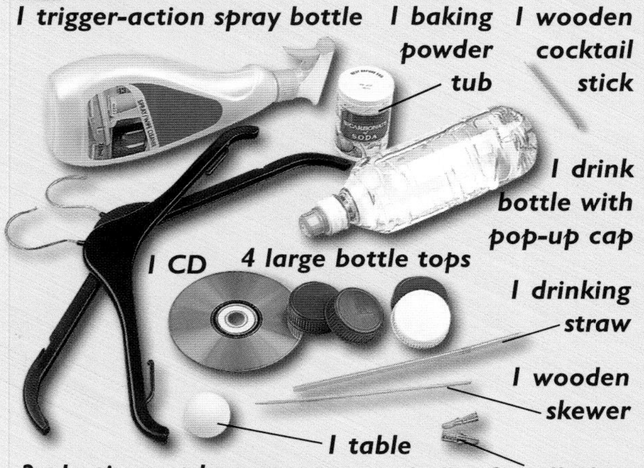

TOOLS

- A junior hacksaw
- Bradawl or an old knitting needle
- Craft knife
- A nightlight
- Glue
- Strong scissors
- Marker pen

! HAZARD

- TAKE CARE WITH THE HOT BRADAWL ON STEPS 1 AND 2 , AND THE SCISSORS AND SHARP EDGES OF THE CD ON STEP10!
- INSTEAD OF USING A CD YOU COULD USE A CIRCLE OF CARD (ABOUT 12CM IN DIAMETER) TO MAKE YOUR SAW BLADE.

YOU'RE IN THE ARMY NOW. WATCH OUT FOR CORPORAL BUZZ! HE'LL CHEW YOU UP AND SPIT YOU OUT. THAT'S WHAT HIS BUZZ BLADE DOES.

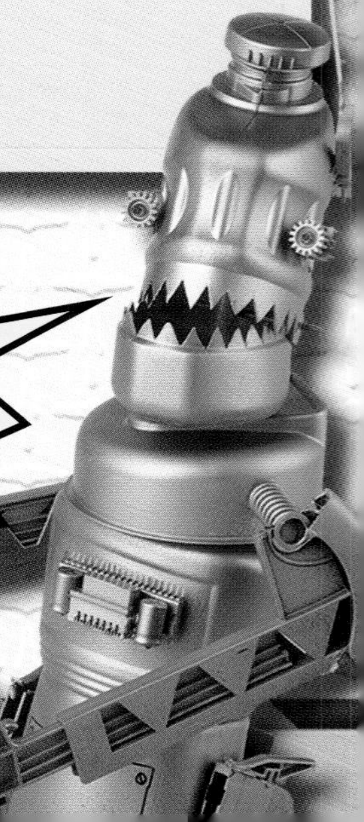

1 Make the main rear wheels by gluing the large bottle tops firmly together in pairs. Poke a hole through the centre of both wheels using the bradawl.

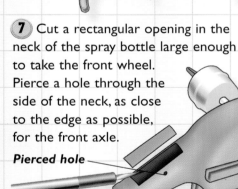

A completed wheel

Large bottle tops

2 Using a heated bradawl poke a hole through the spray bottle as shown. The holes should be about 5cm from the bottom of the bottle. Check that the skewer fits through the holes easily, without sticking in any way.

5cm

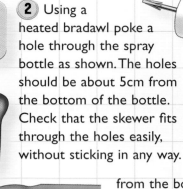

3 Assemble the rear wheels, using a small piece of plastic straw to keep the wheels away from the body. Leave enough skewer at either end to take the wall plugs. Glue the plugs and wheels in place, but make sure the whole axle spins freely.

4 Saw about 12cm from each end of one of your coat hangers to form the mudguards.

Coat hanger mudguard

5 Glue them in place above the rear wheels as shown.

Glue one coat hanger over the top edge of the robot as an armoured spine.

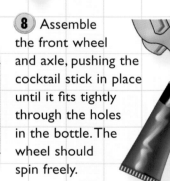

Pierced hole in wheel

6 Cut the bottom centimetre from the baking powder tub and push the top into it, to make a large, narrow wheel. Pierce a hole through the centre of the wheel, large enough to pass a cocktail stick through freely.

7 Cut a rectangular opening in the neck of the spray bottle large enough to take the front wheel. Pierce a hole through the side of the neck, as close to the edge as possible, for the front axle.

Pierced hole

8 Assemble the front wheel and axle, pushing the cocktail stick in place until it fits tightly through the holes in the bottle. The wheel should spin freely.

9 Remove the screw-top from the drink bottle. Put the pop-up cap to one side. You'll need it later. Glue a table tennis ball to the open end of the bottle. Glue the screw-top of the drink bottle to the table tennis ball, at 45°.

Draw a tooth pattern along the edge of a CD with a marker pen.

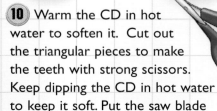

10 Warm the CD in hot water to soften it. Cut out the triangular pieces to make the teeth with strong scissors. Keep dipping the CD in hot water to keep it soft. Put the saw blade somewhere safe, to be fitted later.

Once the paint is dry, fit the saw blade on to its housing and secure it with the pop-up cap that you kept earlier. So how does it feel to have created such a mechanical marvel? You are well on the way to becoming an experienced robot builder. If you have two Robot Warriors, turn to the Battle Bank to try some tactics and manoeuvres. Or carry on bot building!

Add Corporal Buzz's specially designed sticker as shown.

Pop-up cap

ROBODOZER

It's a robot. It's a bulldozer. It's Robodozer! Not only does this robot have the strength of its toothed shovel out front to scoop up the opposition, but on top is a catapulting cage, capable of firing marbles and other small objects right into the heart of the enemies' defences. Wicked wheel spikes will dent and damage other robot body shells as they glance past.

PARTS

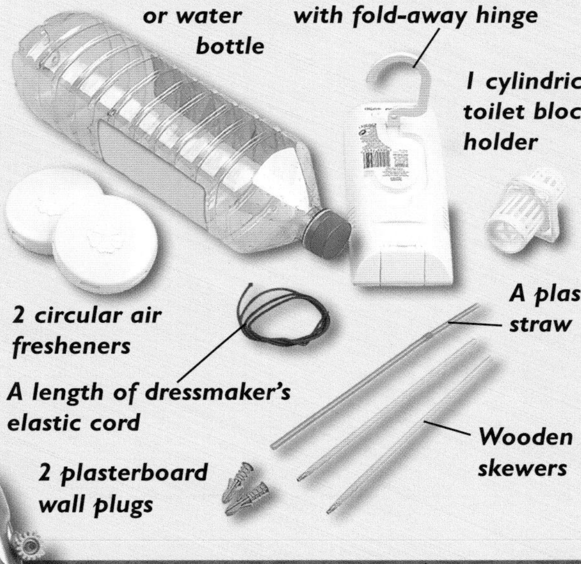

A ribbed juice or water bottle

A flip-top shower gel bottle with fold-away hinge

1 cylindrical toilet block holder

2 circular air fresheners

A length of dressmaker's elastic cord

2 plasterboard wall plugs

A plastic straw

Wooden skewers

TOOLS

- A junior hacksaw
- Bradawl or an old knitting needle
- Craft knife
- Strong scissors
- A nightlight
- Glue

HAZARD

- BE CAREFUL WHEN USING THE HOT BRADAWL ON STEPS 1, 2, AND 8. ALSO BEWARE OF SHARP SCISSORS ON 10!

You'd better well shout – you'd better well cry You'd better watch out – I'm telling you why Robo-dozer's coming to town Robo-dozer's coming to town Ro - bo - do - zer's coming to town!

CHECK OUT THE ELECTRA EXTRA SECTION BEFORE YOU START IF YOU WOULD LIKE TO FIT A MOTOR TO ROBO TO MAKE HIM WHIZZ ALONG!

1 Make a hole each side of your bottle, about 4cm from the back, using a heated bradawl or knitting needle. A skewer should fit easily through the holes so that the rear wheels spin freely.

End taken off holder

4 Cut the hook from the toilet block holder using scissors, then take off the end so that one side is open.

7 Pierce a hole in the catapult arm about halfway up with a heated bradawl. Thread the end of the elastic through the hole. Pull the elastic (not too tight) and tie about two or three knots to secure it.

Hole pierced in catapult arm

10 Cut a section from the ribbed water bottle with your scissors. This should be about seven ribbed sections long and 6cm wide. Snip small triangles from the wider edge. This is Robo's shovel.

2 Separate the two air fresheners and remove the scented disks. Choose the two identical halves with the smaller holes at their centre. Using your bradawl, pierce holes through the centre.

5 Glue the holder into the shower gel bottle hook with the open end facing forwards.

8 Pierce a hole through the body of the robot with your bradawl, next to the spot where the catapult arm is hinged. The hole should go right through the bottle.

11 Glue the shovel to the flip-up flap at the front of your robot. Use a generous blob of glue to fix the plastic shovel in place.

3 Slot the rear wheels on to the axle as shown, fitting a small section of straw (about 5mm) between the robot body and wheel. Leave just enough skewer extending out of the wheel ends so that you can glue a wall plug to each end. Check the wheels spin smoothly and evenly.

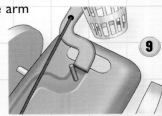

5mm of straw

Wall plug

6 Remove the lid of the bottle and pierce a hole through the side opposite the hinge with your bradawl. Thread one end of the elastic through the hole and tie at least two knots in the end. Put the lid back on so that the elastic is on the top of the robot.

9 Glue a piece of skewer through both holes so that about 2cm sticks up in front of the catapult arm. This will stop the arm from firing too far forward and missing its target.

FINISHING

Give Robodozer a sparkling finish. If the shovel keeps falling off, you can make a stronger joint. Make two holes with a heated bradawl through the shovel and bottle flap. Now glue two short screws or bits of matchstick into the holes, pushing them right through the shovel and into the flap. That should do it! Now grab some marbles and turn to the Battle Bank for a spot of target practice.

Add Robodozer's specially designed sticker as shown.

RAMJET

Built for power and speed, Ramjet can launch himself directly at the approaching contender with all the fury of a charging bull. His body-piercing ram is designed to penetrate even the toughest of armour and inflict maximum damage to the opponent's circuitry within. Extra features include rubber-powered drive shaft and real electronic components.

PARTS

- 2 wooden skewers
- 1 plastic straw
- 1 piece of wooden dowel
- 1 table tennis ball
- Dressmaker's elastic cord
- 1 pen top
- Elastic band
- 1 talcum powder container
- 2 circular air fresheners
- 3 electrical clips
- 1 plasterboard wall plug
- 1 piece of computer circuit board

CHECK OUT THE ELECTRA EXTRA INSTRUCTIONS ON HOW TO GIVE RAMJET MOTORISED BATTERING POWER!

TOOLS

- A junior hacksaw
- Bradawl or an old knitting needle
- Craft knife
- A nightlight
- Glue
- Phillips screwdriver – slightly wider than the dowel

⚠ HAZARD

- YOU SHOULD NEVER BE IN SUCH A HURRY THAT SAFETY COMES SECOND. REMEMBER THE CORRECT ORDER...SAFETY FIRST!

WHEELS THAT SQUEAL AND RAM OF STEEL, THE ENEMY SHOULD WORRY. THEY CAN'T ESCAPE THEIR AWFUL FATE, FROM RAMJET'S MIGHTY FURY!

1 Cut a rectangular hole in one side of the talcum powder container to gain access to the inside. Make holes in either side of the robot body large enough for the dowel to fit through easily.

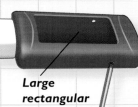

Large rectangular hole

Heated screwdriver

2 Separate two air fresheners and use the two halves with the larger holes at their centre. Use the discarded ones to make Robodozer. Cut a length of dowel about 4cm wider than the body.

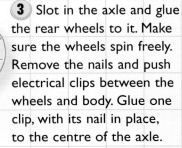

3 Slot in the axle and glue the rear wheels to it. Make sure the wheels spin freely. Remove the nails and push electrical clips between the wheels and body. Glue one clip, with its nail in place, to the centre of the axle.

Electrical clips hold wheels in place

Electrical clip fixed to axle

4 Make a hole in the top of the robot body near the front. Thread your elastic through the hole and tie at least 2 knots in the end.

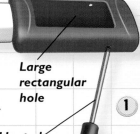

5 Thread enough elastic to reach just past the rear axle, tie a loop in the end and hook it over the electrical clip nail.

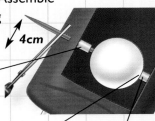

6 Make a hole in the table tennis ball with a heated bradawl so that a skewer fits through easily and the ball spins freely. Push holes into the side of the robot at least 4cm back from the front edge. Assemble the front wheel using pieces of plastic straw as spacers.

Holes through ball (front wheel) to hold axle

Straw spacers stop the table tennis ball from moving sideways

Holes for axle

7 Pierce a hole through the back of the robot close to the top edge and one in the centre of the cap using a heated bradawl.

8 Insert a skewer all the way until it comes out of the front and glue a wall plug on to the skewer. Glue a pen top to the rear of the skewer.

pen top

Wall plug

9 Make a slot across the end of the pen top with the heated bradawl.

Glue the circuit board in place on top of your robot, spray the whole thing and you're in business. To power up Ramjet's elastic motor, hook the elastic over the nail on the back axle. Holding the robot firmly in one hand, wind the rear wheels backwards until the elastic is tight. Now place it on a carpeted or rough surface and let go...

Add Ramjet's specially designed sticker as shown.

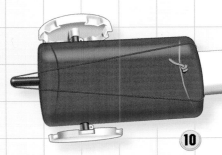

10 Stretch an elastic band over the neck of the bottle and hook it over the slot you made in the pen top. Pull the pen top back, then let go and the ram will operate.

BATTLE BANK

Building a robot is one thing, but learning to operate it is another. So check out the Top Tips panel first and try out your robot operating skills.

Once you have mastered these skills, mark out a Robodrome arena for your battles. Use an indoor floor space or an outdoor patio to compete on. Collect objects, such as the ones shown here, to build obstacles and challenges for each robot. The more robots you have, the more fun your battles will be, so encourage your friends to build their own robots and pit their champions against yours for real head-to-head competitions. Make your own scoreboard or use the scoresheet on page 23.

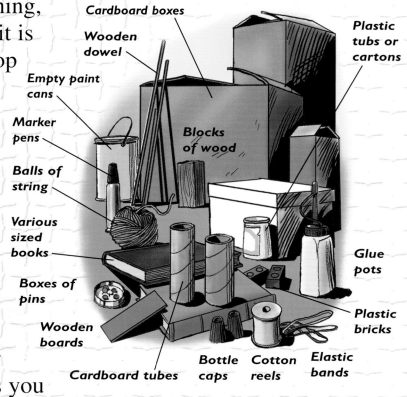

Cardboard boxes
Wooden dowel
Empty paint cans
Marker pens
Balls of string
Various sized books
Boxes of pins
Wooden boards
Cardboard tubes
Bottle caps
Cotton reels
Elastic bands
Plastic bricks
Glue pots
Plastic tubs or cartons
Blocks of wood

TOP TIPS

- Make sure that your robot's wheels are accurately lined up and well-balanced. This will make all the difference in the heat of the battle.
- Practise flipping Hatchet's arm with your thumb.
- Improve your wrist action when spinning Corporal Buzz's saw blade.
- Try out a range of scoops and flips with Doberbot and Robodozer.
- Even a simple mechanism such as Ramjet's elastic powered ram can be very effective if used at just the right moment. Timing is crucial.

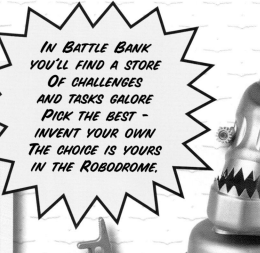

IN BATTLE BANK YOU'LL FIND A STORE OF CHALLENGES AND TASKS GALORE PICK THE BEST – INVENT YOUR OWN THE CHOICE IS YOURS IN THE ROBODROME.

THE ALPHA CHALLENGE

Lay out a long, straight line of string or wool on the ground. You could tape either end in place to stop it from moving. Now see how accurately you can propel your robot along this line without it veering off. To score points, your robot should travel not less than one metre along the line and stay as close as possible to the string. Score 30 points for a perfect finish. Take away 5 points for every centimetre that you stray off course.

THE BETA CHALLENGE

Build a pyramid of cotton reels, each row being one less than the last until you have one bobbin on top. From a distance of 1.5 metres, launch your robot at the wall. Score 5 points for every bobbin knocked down and an extra 10 points if you knock the whole wall down in one go.

Glue two pieces of dowel into board at back

A piece of elastic tied to the dowels makes a catapult

THE GAMMA CHALLENGE

Set up a long distance trial. Mark out a starting line, then see which robot can travel the furthest with one push. Score 50 points for the winning long distance run. Experiment with different ways of launching your robots:
• Push by hand.
• Make a ramp using a piece of thin hardboard to start your robots off.
• Use elastic to motorise all your robot's rear wheels as shown in Ramjet's assembly breakdown.
• Make an elastic robot launcher as shown in the picture.

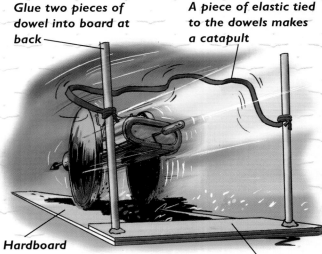

Hardboard runway

Piece of board glued to back of runway

THE DELTA CHALLENGE

Set up a jump course using two ramps. The idea is to see how far your robots can travel. Increase the gap between your ramps until none of your robots can make the distance. Score an increasing number of points for each gap your robot leaps.

10cm ~   5 points
20cm ~ 10 points
30cm ~ 20 points
40cm ~ 40 points
50cm ~ 80 points   And so on...

Either launch your robots by hand or make an elastic launcher as shown in the picture above.

THE EPSILON CHALLENGE

If your robot has a missile launcher, such as the one on Robodozer, then set up some targets to aim for. Targets could either be a row of small objects to knock down or a paper scoring target with points getting higher and a bull's-eye at the centre worth 50 points.

THE ZETA CHALLENGE

To test out the speed of your robots, tie a thin string to the front of each one. For this challenge you will need another person throwing a dice. The dice thrower rolls a dice over and over again until a six is rolled. Once a six has been thrown, the robot must quickly escape by being pulled out of reach before being captured by the dice thrower. The robot is captured by bringing the hand straight down onto the string, preventing its escape. Score 10 points for each successful escape with a maximum of five attempts.

THE ETA CHALLENGE

Attach objects such as marbles to the tops of two robots using small blobs of Blu-Tack or double-sided tape. Bash and crash your robots against each other until one of them loses its marbles! The winner gets 80 points. Robots can use any of their weapons, scoops and special features to help them win in this challenge .

THE THETA CHALLENGE

Set up a goal-scoring challenge. Place two cotton reels on the ground as goalposts. Use a table tennis ball and try to score goals by firing your robot at the ball. Score 30 points for each goal scored. You can make this more challenging by adding a robot goalkeeper. There is a scoresheet for you to photocopy on the opposite page, to keep a record of your scores.

SCORESHEET

ALPHA

BETA

GAMMA

DELTA

EPSILON

ZETA

ETA

THETA

ELECTRA EXTRA

So you think you're a budding sparky? Rubber bands are not good enough eh? Then you're the kind of Roboteer we're looking for at the Robot Centre. With the right components you can achieve electrifying results! Specialist tools are not essential, but you'll find that a pair of proper wire strippers comes in handy. A soldering iron is the best tool for joining wires, but it can get very hot, so you must have adult help. Wires can also be twisted and held in place with electrical tape. Explore your local hobby shop and look at adding zippy motors, coloured lights and noisy buzzers to any of the robots.

TOOLS

- Wire strippers
- Soldering iron
- Electrical tape

HAZARD

- YOU SHOULD ASK AN ADULT TO HELP YOU IF YOU PLAN TO USE A SOLDERING IRON IN THIS SECTION.

PARTS

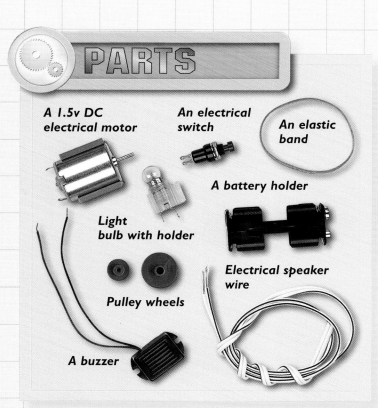

A 1.5v DC electrical motor

An electrical switch

An elastic band

A battery holder

Light bulb with holder

Pulley wheels

Electrical speaker wire

A buzzer

HERE'S A REALLY SUPER TIP, TO GIVE YOUR ROBOTS EXTRA ZIP, ADD MOTORS, LIGHTS AND BUZZERS TOO, WITH ELECTRA EXTRA...IT'S UP TO YOU!

FITTING LIGHTS AND BUZZERS

1 Make a hole in the back of Hatchet's shell with a heated bradawl and fit the switch, securing it with the nut provided.

2 Make a small hole in the front for the two buzzer wires to pass through and glue the buzzer in place.

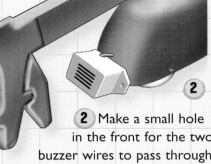

3 Solder two wires onto the switch terminals. Connect one of these to a buzzer wire and the other to one end of the battery.

5 Try fitting a light bulb to dazzle the opposition. But remember, although lights and buzzers are great, the more you fit, the more power you use, so your batteries won't last as long. If you use Light Emitting Diodes (LEDs, which usually come in red and green) then they must be wired up with current flowing in the right direction.

4 Connect the other end of the battery to the other buzzer wire (shown in black in the picture on step 3). As space is so limited, you can do away with a battery holder by soldering wires to the battery. When your battery runs down, just solder another one in to replace it.

FITTING A MOTOR TO CORPORAL BUZZ

1 Push the small pulley wheel firmly onto the motor spindle.

2 Slot the motor into the holder and glue the unit onto the back of Corporal Buzz. Using a holder means that you can adjust the position of the motor once it is in place.

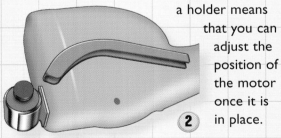

5 Glue the battery holder in place on the back of Corporal Buzz. Make sure there is enough room to remove the batteries when they run down.

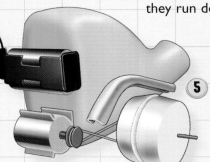

3 Glue the other pulley wheel onto the rear wheel and axle.

6 Connect one strand of the speaker wire to the motor and the other strand to the battery terminal wire. The other battery terminal wire should also be connected directly to the motor.

4 Fit the wheels in place and stretch an elastic band over the two pulley wheels. Putting a twist in the elastic band to form a figure of eight will stop it from slipping off too easily.

7 Connect the other end of the speaker wire to your switch. Solder the wires in place after twisting them onto the terminals.

8

8 You can make a neat switch holder by fitting the switch into a 35mm film container. Make a hole in each end, using a heated bradawl, for the wires and switch. Switches usually have a small nut to hold them in place.

9 Well done! Now you have a simple remote control unit to send your robot into battle, 3-2-1... charge! If you managed that easily and would like to make a more complex remote control unit with forward and reverse capabilities-then stand by for my DIY Remote Control.

9

FITTING MOTORS TO OTHER ROBOTS

BASIC WIRING CIRCUIT FOR FITTING MOTORS

With the other three robots, the basic method of wiring up the motor is shown here. Attach one wire from the battery holder to the motor, twisting it together securely. Attach wires from the motor to the switch and from the switch back to the battery holder to form a circuit. A soldering iron will make much better connections, but ask an adult to help you.

RAMJET

Pulley wheel   Elastic band   **Motor**

Wires   **Batteries**

HATCHET

For Hatchet and Ramjet, glue the motor inside the body shell as shown in the diagrams. Robodozer and Corporal Buzz work best if you fix the motor to the outside of the body shell at the back. The axle pulley wheel is also on the outside for both of these robots.

 TOP TIPS

- Unfortunately, Doberbot cannot be motorised easily. If you want him to have a motor you will need to redesign his wheels so that they have an axle. But hey! How about wiring up LEDs to give Doberbot some super glow-in-the-dark red eyes? (See Fitting Lights and Buzzers, on page 25.)
- If possible, glue the battery holder inside your robot so it is out of the way. Glue motors so that the motor pulley wheel lines up with the pulley wheel on the axle (see diagrams above).
- Make sure you use the right size elastic band so it is quite tight, but not so tight that the wheels don't turn.
- If your robot moves back instead of forwards, don't panic. Remove the elastic band, twist it to make a figure of eight and put it back on. Your robot will now move forwards. This is easier than undoing the wires and changing the direction of the current.

Motor fits on back   **ROBODOZER**

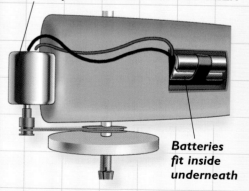

Batteries fit inside underneath

On Hatchet and Ramjet, put an elastic band over the pulley before you fit the axle. Leave one wheel unglued so you can replace broken bands easily. Corporal Buzz and Robodozer can have elastic bands fitted later.

DIY REMOTE CONTROL SWITCH

If you're feeling really adventurous, how about building your own two-way switch in a hand-held controller. This controller can also hold the batteries to power your robot, so there's no need to fit them to the body shell. Here's how to do it.

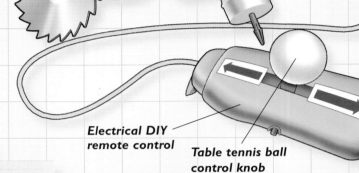

Electrical DIY remote control

Table tennis ball control knob

PARTS

A flat bottle such as a shower gel bottle

Electrical speaker wire

An elastic band

A table tennis ball

A coat hanger

8 brass paper fasteners

A wooden skewer

TOOLS

- Bradawl or an old knitting needle
- Glue
- Strong scissors
- Craft knife
- Junior hacksaw

TO START 'EM UP IN HALF A TICK,
A SIMPLE SWITCH MIGHT DO THE TRICK.
REMOTE CONTROL IS MUCH MORE FUN,
SO WHY NOT CHECK OUT HOW IT'S DONE?

⚠ HAZARD

- SOME STEPS IN THE DIY REMOTE CONTROL SECTION ARE FIDDLY AND CAN BE HAZARDOUS, SO MAKE SURE YOU ASK AN ADULT TO HELP YOU.
- THE SAFETY WARNINGS GIVEN SO FAR FOR ALL THE PROJECTS IN THIS MANUAL APPLY TO THE USE OF TOOLS HERE. PLEASE CHECK THEM AGAIN AND PUT SAFETY FIRST.

ASSEMBLY

1 Cut a slot 5cm long and 1.5cm wide in each flat side of the shower gel bottle. Then pierce holes in the sides of the bottle, as shown, using a heated bradawl. The holes should line up exactly with the centres of the slots.

5cm

1

Pierce holes on both sides of the bottle

2 Remove one arm from the skirt hanger and saw off the end to make a control stick at least 12cm long. Pierce a hole halfway along using a heated bradawl.

2

3

12cm

3 Push a wooden skewer through the side holes of the bottle and control stick. Snip off the ends of the skewer so that about half a centimetre sticks out of each side.

4 Hook an elastic band over the two skewer ends across the bottle. There should be elastic on either side of the control arm so that it springs back to a vertical position when released.

4

5 Cut a slot in the table tennis ball with a warmed craft knife. Glue the ball to the sawn off end of the control arm (see picture on page 27).

5

6

6 Glue the four brass paper fasteners onto the control arm head, pointing diagonally downwards as shown.

7 Rock the arm forwards and with a marking pen mark the points where each of the four fasteners touch the surface of the bottle.

7

8 Pierce holes with the bradawl where you made marks with the pen. The holes should be large enough to push brass fasteners through easily.

8

9 Strip the plastic from the ends of four lengths of wire. Two should be about 20cm long and the other two 12cm. Attach each wire to a paper fastener. Push the wires through the holes and out through the open neck of the bottle. The two shorter wires should be fed through the holes nearest to the neck.

9

Wire with end stripped away

10 To remember which wire is which, put a black dot on one paper fastener head and a black line around the other end of the wire. The next fastener would have two dots on its head and two bands on the end of the wire and so on.

10

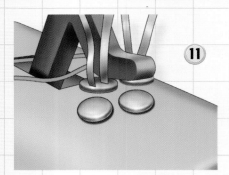

11 Press the fasteners into their holes and secure each one with a blob of glue. Be careful not to get glue on the tops of the brass heads themselves.

12 Glue a battery holder to the bottom of the bottle. It is easier to replace batteries if this stays on the outside.

13 Attach the two battery wires to the nearest two heads on the control arm. Solder or tape the wires to hold them in place.

14 Fasten two short wires across the control arm head as shown. Make sure you cross them over to reverse the polarity of the battery to the other wires to give you reverse gear. Solder or tape the wires to the brass fasteners, making sure there is a good contact.

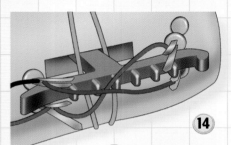

15 Take a long controller wire (speaker wire is best) and thread it through the bottle top. Twist the long and short wires on each side of the controller arm together to make a pair of leads. Twist a wire from the long controller lead to each of the pairs of leads.

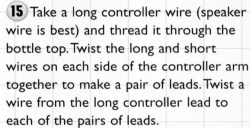

Electrical tape

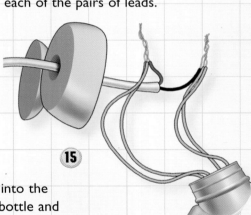

16 Stick a piece of electrical tape over the twisted wires so the bare ends are totally covered.

17 Push the wires into the neck of the bottle and replace the lid.

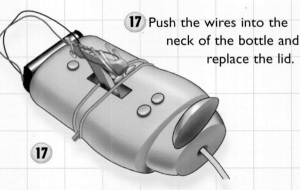

FINISHING

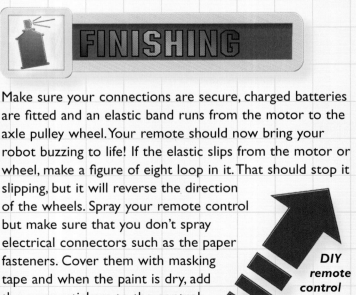

18 Connect the two long controller wires to the robot motor and secure them in place with solder. You could use crocodile clips if you don't want the wires to be connected permanently.

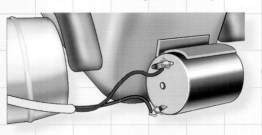

Make sure your connections are secure, charged batteries are fitted and an elastic band runs from the motor to the axle pulley wheel. Your remote should now bring your robot buzzing to life! If the elastic slips from the motor or wheel, make a figure of eight loop in it. That should stop it slipping, but it will reverse the direction of the wheels. Spray your remote control but make sure that you don't spray electrical connectors such as the paper fasteners. Cover them with masking tape and when the paint is dry, add the arrow stickers to the control stick (see picture on page 27).

DIY remote control arrow sticker

NEW GENERATION

If you've had fun making the robots so far, then don't stop here. You have learned new skills and techniques so why not use them to design and build your own robots?

Don't forget, that for a first-class Roboteer anything is possible – and it all starts with an idea. Remember to use your tools carefully and put safety first at all times.

I hope you have enjoyed your training and studies so far. Keep practising those manoeuvres in the Robodrome, and farewell for now, Roboteers!

WEBSITES

The internet is an exciting way to search for information on robots. There are books for sale on robot construction, video clips, photos and much more. Here are a few of my favourite websites:

www.robotbooks.com
A great collection of books and links on robot hobbies and clubs. Click on 'Robolinks' too.

www.robotics.nasa.gov
Nasa's official site for all that's robotic.

www.robosaurus.com
Check out the world's only 40 foot car-munching monsterbot – great photos, info and video clips!

www.robotcombat.com
Links to battling robot competitions and TV shows.

www.robotwars.co.uk
The official UK website of the BBC's Robotwars.

www.battlebots.com
The official US website of Comedy Central's Battlebots.

www.robotbuilders.net
Serious robot construction based on famous film robots.

DESIGN TOP TIPS

● Search out strange and unusual plastic bottles and containers around your home. Weird shapes will fire your imagination when you start designing.

● Be creative with different shapes and sizes of circular plastic tops and containers to make your robot's wheels.

● Look out for small plastic bits and bobs such as pen tops and broken toy parts. Then you can use these in your design so that your robot stands out from the rest in the Robodrome.

● Experiment with paint effects and other finishing touches. Use oil or acrylic based model paints to decorate your robots as well as spray paints. Personalise your robot by designing your own stickers.

IF YOU'VE REACHED THE END AND MADE THE GRADE WELL DONE! CONGRATULATIONS! YOU'RE READY NOW TO TRY YOUR HAND AT AN 'ALL-NEW GENERATION'.

I WISH YOU WELL, YOUNG ROBOTEERS AND LAST FAREWELLS I BID, SO, BON VOYAGE AND CHEERIO YOURS TRULY, CYBER SID!

GLOSSARY

Alpha (beta, gamma, delta, epsilon, zeta, eta, theta) – letters of the Greek alphabet.

Acrylic paint – resin-based paint that can be diluted with water.

CD – compact disc

Circuit board – a thin board containing electrical components (parts) and circuits.

Crocodile clips – small metal clips with teeth that can be used to join wires together.

Diameter – the distance from one edge of a circle to the other, across the centre.

Electrical circuit – components that work when electricity flows through them, usually from one pole of a battery to the other.

Electrical clips – small plastic clips with a small nail in them, used to fix wires and cables to walls.

Electrical motor (1.5v DC) – a small machine that runs on battery power. The '**v**' stands for volts, and shows the strength of electrical current. **DC** stands for direct current, where the electricity flows in one direction from one pole of the battery to the other pole.

Electrical tape – Also called insulation tape. Sticky, stretchy tape used for wrapping around bare wires to stop them from touching other wires and interfering with your circuit. As a safer alternative to soldering you can twist wires together firmly and cover the ends with small pieces of the tape.

LEDs – Light Emitting Diodes. Small electrical components that glow – usually green or red. These will only glow when the electricity is flowing in the right direction. You will have to experiment to find out which way works and which doesn't.

Manoeuvres – a series of movements requiring skill and care.

Mechanism – a set of moving parts that work together.

Motorise – to add a motor.

Nightlight – a small, safety candle in a metal holder.

Phillips screwdriver – screwdriver with a narrow star-shaped end rather than a wide, flat end.

Robodrome – a specially designed arena or stadium for battling robots and challenges of skill.

Soldering – joining wires or metal surfaces using a soldering iron. The soldering iron is used to melt and apply the solder (a mixture of two or more metals) to the surfaces that need joining.

Sparky – a nickname for an electrician.

Wall plugs – small, plastic parts for fixing screws into walls.

Wooden skewer – a long, thin piece of wood for holding food together in cooking.

First published in Great Britain in 2001 by The Chicken House, 2 Palmer Street, Frome, Somerset BA11 IDS Email chickenhouse@doublecluck.com
Text © Stephen Munzer 2001 Stephen Munzer has asserted his rights under the Copyright, Designs and Patents Act, 1988, to be identified as the author of this work. All rights reserved. No part of this publication may be reproduced or transmitted or utilised in any form or by any means, electronic, mechanical or otherwise, without prior permission of the Publisher.

Designed and produced exclusively for The Chicken House by Oyster Books Ltd.
Printed and bound by Lee Fung Asco, China

Designers: Bean Bog Frag Book Design
Illustrators: Push Creative, Roger Goode, Roger Wade-Walker
Photography by Simon Powell

A CIP catalogue record for this book is available from the British Library